The
CRYSTAL
HEALING
Journal

Your Personal Journey
Towards Healing

summersdale

THE CRYSTAL HEALING JOURNAL

Text by Susan McCann

An Hachette UK Company
www.hachette.co.uk

Summersdale Publishers Ltd
Part of Octopus Publishing Group Limited
Carmelite House
50 Victoria Embankment
LONDON
EC4Y 0DZ
UK

www.summersdale.com

Printed and bound in China

ISBN: 978-1-80007-677-8

Name:

....

Date of birth:

....

Journal start date:

....

Favourite crystal:

....

Goals for your crystal healing journey:

....

....

....

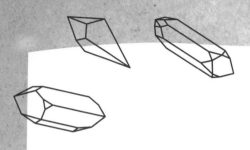

INTRODUCTION

Once you discover the joy and power of working with crystals, you'll want to have them around you every day. They've been used by human civilization for millennia, for everything from healing and predicting the future to colourful eye makeup.

The Crystal Healing Journal will guide you through the essential facts you need to know about working with crystals, including how to look after them, how to choose them, and tips on cleansing and charging.

Thirty of the most essential stones are featured in succinct profiles, arranged to reflect balance and variation, with two pages of handy prompts to journal your experiences of each crystal.

Toward the end of this book you'll find your very own Healing Journal, where you can record further experiences with any of the profiled crystals, or others of your choice.

This healing journey belongs to you, and may it bring you joy, self-discovery and well-being!

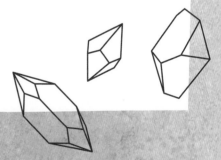

A BRIEF HISTORY OF CRYSTAL HEALING

Crystals have been on earth since the beginning of time. Follow the timeline below for an insight into how crystals have been used throughout history for healing and protection by different cultures.

2.5 million years ago
Ancient people in East Asia adorned the eyes of statues with Aventurine, a translucent form of Quartz, believing it would increase the statue's visionary powers.

4500–2000 BCE
The Ancient Sumerians, one of the first civilizations, performed incantations and rituals with crystals to ward off bad spirits. They also made healing essences using crystals.

3500 BCE
In Ancient Mesopotamia (modern day Iraq), Agate was a symbol of strength and Haematite was used to cool the blood.

Ancient China
Agate was thought to energize a person's chi and purify the mind.

Ancient Japan
Clear Quartz was regarded as a symbol of perfection, because it was thought to be a white dragon's breath in physical form. Dragons represented generosity and benevolence in Japanese mythology, so the crystal became associated with these values too.

Ancient Byzantine and Assyria

Carnelian was used for courage, especially in battle. It was also thought to inspire public speaking, helping the performer to speak fearlessly and eloquently.

Ancient Egypt

Carnelian was called the "setting sun" by the Ancient Egyptians and was believed to energize the spirit and body. It formed part of King Tut's decorated breastplate and death mask. Carnelian's orange-red colour meant that it was linked to the fertile menstrual blood of the mother goddess, Isis.

Lapis Lazuli was used as blue eyeshadow by Cleopatra, and also in death masks as it was thought to guide souls into the afterlife.

Clear Quartz was used to build monuments, as it was thought to channel energy from the planetary system, while grey-black Haematite was used to treat inflammation because of its iron oxide content.

Ancient Greece and Rome

Bloodstone amulets were worn by Ancient Greeks and Ancient Romans to boost endurance and physical strength during athletic competitions and displays. The stone was thought to protect against injury and disease, and was commonly dipped in cold water and placed on the body to promote healing and improve circulation.

Native America

Native Americans in the Warner Valley of Oregon, USA, have always collected Sunstone.

In Native American legend, a great warrior was wounded by an arrow and Sunstone is said to have soaked up his blood, resulting in its subsequent orange-flecked colour and infusing the stone with the warrior's spirit.

Native American cultures treated crystals with utmost respect and they were collected by healers and diviners, who used them for healing and rituals. Turquoise was especially precious to them and was used in ceremonies to bring protection and even rain.

South American cultures

Mayan natives believed Clear Quartz crystal skulls held their ancestors' spirits.

c. 350 CE

St Epiphanius, Bishop of Salamis in Cyprus, wrote a treatise titled *De Duodecim Lapidibus* (On Twelve Stones). It discusses the 12 stones in the Bible said to have adorned Aaron's breastplate and ascribes healing qualities to each one.

The Vikings (800–1066 CE)

Ancient Norse texts suggest Vikings used Norwegian Sunstone to navigate the seas. The tiny particles of Haematite in Sunstone shimmer in the light, meaning the Vikings were able to use it to gauge the position of the sun.

Medieval period (fifth to fourteenth century)

To ensure a good harvest in the medieval era, Agate was tied to the horns of oxen. Agate was thought to quell thunder and lightning storms.

c. 1067–1081

Marbod, Bishop of Rennes, wrote *De Lapidibus* (On Stones), describing 60 gemstones and their healing properties.

Middle Ages (1154–1485)

Christians in Europe during the Middle Ages linked Bloodstone to the crucifixion of Christ, giving the stone a sacred power. They believed the blood from Christ's wounds dripped onto the dark green earth and turned to stone. This is how Bloodstone acquired its name and is the reason this crystal is believed to have exceptional wound-healing powers.

Crystal balls made of Clear Quartz were used in the Middle Ages by European clairvoyants to predict the future.

Age of Enlightenment
(seventeenth and eighteenth centuries)

In 1659, *Gemmarius Fidelius* (The Faithful Lapidary) was published by Thomas Nicols. He denounced crystals, saying they didn't possess any healing properties, prompting the use of precious stones for healing and protection to fall from favour in Europe.

1800s

A time of scepticism around crystal healing. Investigations into bogus mediums led to cynicism regarding crystal and faith healers. Advances in science and medicine meant people switched to new medicines.

Modern times

New Age culture arrived in the 1970s, bringing a revival of crystals for healing practices. Books based on old traditions about the use of crystals for spiritual well-being re-emerged.

Now in the twenty-first century, crystal healing is accepted as a mainstream and complementary therapy, crossing the boundaries of religious, scientific and spiritual beliefs.

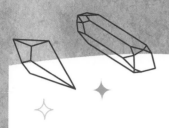

HOW CRYSTALS WORK

Some still see spirituality and science as two separate concepts, but there is a scientific basis behind the way crystals work.

Everything in our universe is made of energy and crystals have naturally occurring energy fields, just like humans do. Humans emit different types of energies depending on how we're feeling. We give out low vibrations when we're feeling down, and frenzied, spiky vibrations if we're stressed. Crystals come from the earth and have very pure, natural high vibration frequencies. When a crystal comes into an environment or into our energy field, it has the effect of balancing and soothing the energies it comes into contact with.

Crystals contain both piezoelectric and pyroelectric properties, meaning they conduct heat and electricity, which causes them to vibrate. This vibrational energy can be harnessed to help restore the body's natural balance and healing mechanisms, as the crystals tune and raise our frequencies. This type of non-invasive healing is called vibrational medicine.

Our forebears have been aware of the healing abilities of crystals for millennia and their properties are mentioned in many early medical texts, with comprehensive records of their use, particularly in Ancient Chinese medicine.

The way in which a crystal is created will have an effect on how it works with your energy field, as will the crystal's colour; colours emit their own energy frequencies and are linked to specific energy centres, known as chakras, in humans.

Crystals are formed by nature in different ways. Some are created by lava and others smoothed by millennia of water erosion. Others are formed in layers over time, creating a banded stone like Agate or Malachite. These banded stones often work to peel away the different layers of emotional debris in the human energy field, as suggested by their layered formation.

HOW TO CHOOSE YOUR CRYSTALS

You can choose which crystals you would like to work with in a variety of ways:

- Intuitively

- According to the known healing properties of a specific crystal

- According to the crystal's colour and associated chakra

Choose your crystals intuitively

One of the easiest ways to choose a crystal is simply by noticing which one catches your eye. Many people have described being drawn to a specific crystal or feel that one seems to be glittering more brightly and standing out more than the rest.

You can also touch and handle the crystal to see how it makes you feel when you are holding it. Does it give you a pleasant feeling and can you feel its energy coursing through you?

The crystal you are the most drawn to will be the correct one for you to be working with at that time.

Choose your crystal according to its specific healing properties

Each type of crystal has a unique set of healing properties associated with it. For example, if you're looking to increase your confidence, you may choose a Citrine. If you're looking to attract love, you may select a Rose Quartz or if you need help with insomnia, Amethyst would be an excellent choice.

Choose your crystal according to its colour and associated chakra

The colours of the crystal are important, as each colour carries its own energy frequency that is linked to one of the seven chakra centres.

- **Red or black:** associated with the grounding energies of the root chakra

- Orange: associated with the sacral chakra and creativity and sexuality

- Yellow: linked to the solar plexus and resonates with confidence

- **Green and pink:** the colours of heart frequency

- **Blue:** relates to communication and the throat chakra

- **Indigo:** associated with the third eye and vision and intuition

- **Purple or white:** the colour frequencies of the crown chakra, which connects you to your spirituality and the higher dimensions

HOW TO CLEANSE
YOUR CRYSTALS

Cleansing your crystals (especially when you first bring them home) is important as they may be holding negative energies from a previous environment or user. Keeping your crystals regularly cleansed to dissolve negative energies from your own environment and practice will help them to work at their best.

Remember to consider the crystal type and colour when cleansing. Some crystals are more fragile than others and not all methods are suitable for each one.

Smudging

Light some white sage or scented wood (for example palo santo, available in any crystal store) and purify the crystal by passing it through the smoke. Always take care when using fire and only perform smudging in a ventilated space.

Sound

Sound frequency moves energy through the crystal. Tuning forks, classical music, singing bowls or tingshas (small cymbals, easily available online) are ideal.

Water

Crystals can be submerged or held under running water for a few minutes to wash away negativity.

Note that soft, fragile stones such as Selenite or Iron Pyrite dissolve, scratch or rust in water.

CHARGING CRYSTALS

Like a battery, crystals need to be recharged after use. Cleanse your crystals first and then recharge them with sun, moon or earth energy.

Charge with moon energy

Let your crystals absorb the moonlight from a windowsill or place them in your garden overnight (you may want to keep them dry and scratch-free on a soft cloth or tray).

Charging in moonlight is suitable for all crystals.

Charge with sun energy

Some crystals thrive on sun energy while others fade easily. The colour properties of each crystal form part of their particular frequency and healing powers, so if their colour fades, their powers may diminish. You can leave darker or fire-coloured crystals, such as Ruby or Tiger's Eye, out in the sun without concern but lighter-coloured crystals such as Turquoise, Aquamarine or Green Fluorite fade easily. These can be put on a windowsill out of direct sunlight, or charged with moon or earth energy instead. Although it may not feel like it, sun energy is still present on a cloudy day so crystals can be charged in sunlight all year round.

Charge with earth energy

Crystals came from the earth, so placing them back underground for a while (anything from a few days to a month) can be extremely nurturing and provide them with some much-needed TLC. Some crystals may be prone to water damage or scratching, so you may want to place them in a small wooden box. Try marking the spot with a garden ornament or a broken piece of plant pot to help you remember where you buried them.

HOW TO TUNE IN TO YOUR CRYSTAL

It's important that you know how to "tune in" and connect with your crystal in order to work with it most effectively. The more you work together, the stronger your communication and rapport will become, just as it would with a friend.

Here are some easy ways to tune in to your crystal:

- Find a quiet space and hold your crystal in your left hand. Look at it closely, noting its colour, shape and texture in detail. Close your eyes and allow yourself to be surrounded by its colour energy.

- Visualize yourself inside the crystal and feel its energy wash over you.

- Place the crystal over your heart to connect it to your heart centre.

Programme your crystal

You can also programme your crystal, meaning that you set an intention on how you'd like it to work with you. This allows you to work toward a specific purpose or goal together, harnessing the crystal's energies toward what you'd like to achieve. It's always important, however, to ask a crystal to work for the highest good of all concerned, so that the crystal never acts on a wrong thought or intention.

Unless you reprogramme your crystal and ask it to help you in a different way, each time you reconnect with your crystal, it will continue to work with you in the way you've asked it to.

How to programme your crystal:

- Find somewhere quiet and relax, holding your crystal in the left hand. Close your eyes.

- Tune in to your crystal as described on the previous page, and then set your intention on how you'd like it to work with you, being as clear and specific as you can. For example: "I would like this Smoky Quartz to assist me with grounding myself."

- Thank the crystal and place it over your heart centre.

Crystals can be programmed with multiple intentions to help you in a variety of ways. They can also work independently in your best interests to bring anything that needs healing to your attention.

How to Look After Your Crystals

Crystals should be stored with care, as they are fragile. Some are made of softer minerals than others, making them prone to scratching and breaking, while some are susceptible to fading in sunlight.

Crystals should be stored separately, so they don't scratch each other, except for tumbled stones (small polished stones found in gem shops), which are more robust and can be kept together.

A box with some soft cloth could be used, preferably with something to separate each crystal, such as a ridge of cloth or glued strips of cardboard.

Lighter-coloured crystals should be kept somewhere dark or shady, while darker-coloured crystals can be kept out for display.

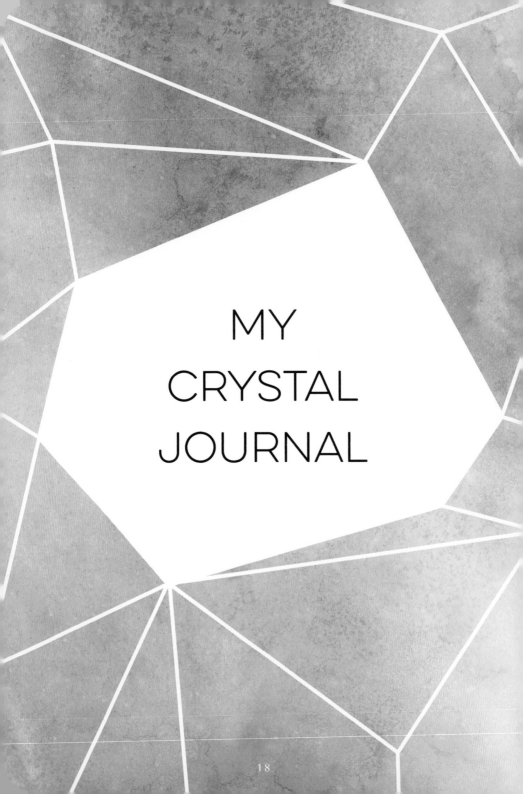

MY
CRYSTAL
JOURNAL

Citrine

Appearance: Yellow, yellow-brown, smoky grey-brown. Natural Citrine is a pale yellow colour, but the majority of Citrine found online and in shops is heat-treated Quartz, which is a darker yellow-brown and is usually found in clusters or points.
Healing properties: Improves confidence and creativity; brings prosperity
Vibe: Energizing and joyful
Associated chakras: Solar plexus, sacral

Citrine is a master at clearing negative energy and replacing it with a positive outlook. Known as the Merchant's Stone, it's a stone of success and can help you to increase your wealth and maintain it. It helps artists unleash their creative energy as it encourages the imagination and boosts self-esteem for healthy creative expression.

Spreading joy and generosity, optimistic Citrine can bring light where there is depression, fear or phobias. Its bright energy can also help with Chronic Fatigue Syndrome, and menstrual and menopausal issues.

Citrine is an excellent stone for manifestation.

Care instructions:

Keep Citrine out of sunlight, as it fades.

Tips for use in healing:

Work with Citrine on your solar plexus to improve confidence. Use an affirmation such as "I choose to be confident" and make it a regular practice so that your confidence levels increase and maintain themselves over time.

For assistance with manifesting wealth, choose a powerful affirmation such as "I manifest wealth and abundance" while you work with your Citrine.

How did you work with this crystal? (e.g. for meditation, using affirmations, or to heal a specific physical or emotional issue)

....

....

How effective did you find Citrine for the above purpose?

....

....

What feelings did the Citrine elicit in you?

....

....

....

How did your confidence levels feel after working with this stone?

....

....

....

....

How did Citrine's sunny energies affect you?

....

....

....

Did you feel any effect or sensations in your physical body from working with this crystal?

....

....

....

Are there any creative projects you need Citrine's assistance with?

....

....

....

Are there any affirmations you would like to work with next time you use Citrine?

....

....

....

Rose Quartz

Appearance: Pink
Healing properties: Heals heartache
and attracts love; promotes
forgiveness and unconditional love
Vibe: Gentle and reassuring
Associated chakra: Heart

This beautiful crystal opens the heart, allowing it to trust again, and is known as the stone of unconditional love. An expert in healing heartache, it can attract new love for those who are single and promote unconditional love for those who are already a pair.

Rose Quartz also encourages you to love and value yourself, supporting self-forgiveness and gently healing any grief.

Rose Quartz is reassuring in times of trauma and makes an ideal stone for use in mid-life crisis as it helps with accepting change.

Care instructions:

Rose Quartz can fade in sunlight.

Tips for use in healing:

For a quick pick-me-up when you're feeling low, place Rose Quartz over your heart and visualize the rose-pink vibes surrounding you with love.

To attract love or promote harmony in an existing relationship, place in the far right-hand corner of the bedroom.

If you need help with self-love, carrying a Rose Quartz in the shape of a heart can provide soothing support.

Were there any specific emotional issues that you needed help with?

....

....

....

How did you work with this crystal? (e.g. meditation, affirmations, placed over heart)

....

How did the energies of Rose Quartz make you feel?

....

Did you receive any images or visions while working with this crystal?

....

....

....

....

Did you receive any advice or guidance from your crystal?

....

....

....

....

Has Rose Quartz changed your perspective on anything?

....

....

....

Have you considered placing Rose Quartz in your living space, and if so, where? What would you like it to help you with in your daily life?

....

....

....

How would you like to work with Rose Quartz next time?

....

....

....

Iron Pyrite

Appearance: Gold to brown, metallic lustre
Healing properties: Boosts self-esteem;
lifts mood; protects against negative energy;
encourages financial and career success
Vibe: Energizing and motivational
Associated chakra: Solar plexus

Dynamic Iron Pyrite will whip you into shape in no time and point you toward achievement. A great stone for success in business, it'll bolster your confidence and flood you with ideas to help you reach your full potential.

Pyrite is known to protect your environment from negative energy, and its sunny outlook can dissipate anxiety. These mood-lifting energies are ideal for helping you to focus on your goals, and Pyrite is the perfect companion to support recovery from fatigue and depression.

Also known as Fool's Gold, Pyrite teaches you that "all that glitters is not gold", and it can help you to see things as they truly are.

Care instructions:

Do not cleanse in water, as Pyrite rusts.

Tips for use in healing:

Place your Pyrite on a desk at work to energize the area around it and promote success in business.

Try manifestation with Pyrite to help make your long-term prosperity goals a reality. Find a quiet space and envision a clear image of whatever you'd like to manifest in your life – from money to a new car. As you inhale, say an affirmation out loud, such as "I choose abundance" or "I am grateful for the abundance in my life" and as you exhale, release any limiting beliefs. Contemplate for at least 20 minutes.

How did you work with Iron Pyrite? (e.g. for manifestation, meditation)

....

Draw your Iron Pyrite below:

Did you ask Pyrite to help you with any particular goals?

....

....

....

....

Did Pyrite lift your mood, and if so, how did it leave you feeling?

....

....

....

Did Pyrite help you to feel more confident and focused on your goals?

....

....

....

Did Pyrite reveal any hidden truths to you?

....

....

....

Do you intend to continue working with Pyrite, and if so, how will you work with it next time?

....

....

....

....

Turquoise

Appearance: Turquoise, green or blue
Healing properties: Protective; purifying;
promotes health and well-being
Vibe: Soothing and calm
Associated chakra: Throat

Turquoise helps you to focus on your health and well-being and is an excellent overall healer. Connected to water energy, this regenerative stone will be your life coach.

Strongly protective, it cleanses negative energy, soothes inflammation and calms emotions.

Turquoise can give the wearer mental strength and self-awareness, helping to prevent self-sabotage. Its rejuvenating properties are ideal for exhaustion and depression, and it can help with panic attacks. It can be used for healing of the whole body and strengthens the immune system.

Care instructions:

Turquoise is prone to fading in direct sunlight and excessive heat. Sensitive to cosmetics.

Tips for use in healing:

Turquoise heightens meditation when placed on the third eye. Work with Turquoise on the throat chakra to help release any barriers to communication and facilitate self-expression.

How did you choose to work with Turquoise? (e.g. meditation)

....

....

What was your intention for the session? Was there anything that you wanted Turquoise to help you heal?

....

....

....

....

Did you feel any sensations in your body or energy field while working with the crystal?

....

....

....

....

What effect did Turquoise have on your mood?

....

....

What did you visualize while working with Turquoise, and did you see any images in your head?

....

....

....

Did Turquoise offer a message or feeling of support?

....

....

....

Did the crystal bring to your awareness something you had not previously realized?

....

....

....

How will you use Turquoise in the future?

....

....

....

Jasper

Appearance: Red, brown, yellow, green, blue, purple. Sometimes patterned
Healing properties: Nurtures and stabilizes during periods of stress
Vibe: Earthy, grounding, energizing
Associated chakras: All, depending on type

Jasper comes in many different colours and patterns and is known as the ultimate nurturing stone. It will help to ground you during times of stress, absorbing negative energy and offering support during conflict. Jasper brings courage, helping you to kick-start your imagination and see your ideas through to fruition with determination. Ideal for support during periods of prolonged illness or hospitalization, it helps to re-energize the body.

Popular types of Jasper include Red, which is excellent for work with the root chakra; Yellow, which is full of positive energy and good for the solar plexus chakra; and Kambaba or Crocodile, which connects with earth energy and the natural world.

Care instructions:

Avoid prolonged exposure to heat as this can cause Jasper to change colour.

Tips for use in healing:

Stroking a piece of Red Jasper can soothe the emotions.
If you're feeling off balance, hold Jasper in your hand and imagine it filling your aura with grounding and balancing energies.

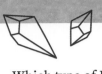

Which type of Jasper did you use?

....

....

....

Did you ask it to work with you in a specific way, or did you allow the crystal to bring the most useful and appropriate thing to the surface for your awareness?

....

....

....

How were you feeling before you worked with Jasper?

....

....

....

How did you feel after working with Jasper?

....

....

....

....

....

Do you feel more connected to the earth and Mother Nature after having worked with this stone?

....

Did you see any images while working with this stone?

....

....

....

What did Jasper teach you?

....

....

....

Do you intend to experiment with other types of Jasper, so that you can see or feel their similarities and differences? If so, research and list other potential Jaspers that you might wish to work with and state why.

....

....

....

....

....

....

Amethyst

Appearance: Purple
Healing properties: Eases grief,
anxiety, insomnia, headaches;
helpful for overcoming addiction
Vibe: Tranquilizing, spiritual
Associated chakras: Crown, third eye

One of nature's most soothing crystals, Amethyst can lull you to sleep or ease a tension headache. Peaceful in the face of anger, it dissipates anxiety and its calming rays can help to process grief.

Amethyst has a highly spiritual vibration that enhances connection to the psychic realms and it can also be a comforting stone for those about to transition through death.

Amethyst is a great support to those battling addiction or trying to overcome obstacles. It helps to stabilize mood and bring hope.

Care instructions:

Amethyst fades in sunlight. Should not be used by those experiencing paranoia or schizophrenia.

Tips for use in healing:

Place under the pillow to aid sleep.

Imagine the soothing rays of Amethyst filling your energy field to bring instant tranquillity.

Place the stone on your third eye to tap into your intuition.

How did you choose to work with Amethyst?

....

What effect did the colour of the Amethyst have on you?

....

Did you feel Amethyst working in any particular areas of your body or energy field?

....

....

....

How were you feeling before you worked with this crystal?

....

....

....

How did you feel afterward?

....

....

....

Did you ask Amethyst to work with you in a particular way, or did you allow it to work generally in your energy field?

....

....

How do you feel about the soothing properties of this stone? Were they effective for you?

....

....

....

Would you recommend using this crystal to others?

....

....

Note down any images or other valuable experiences that arose from your work with Amethyst:

....

....

....

....

Ruby

Appearance: Red
Healing properties: Promotes courage and leadership; activates and balances the heart; stimulates life force and passion
Vibe: Energizing and dynamic
Associated chakras: Root, heart

Associated with fire and sun energy, warm Ruby inspires a zest for life and stimulates passion. It opens and balances the heart, promoting joy and clearing anger and negative energy.

Ruby boosts leadership skills, sharpening the mind and fostering courage and strength. It is a motivational stone that helps you to set and achieve realistic goals.

Ruby is a stone of abundance, helping the bearer to retain both wealth and passion, and its vigorous flow is beneficial for the heart and circulatory system. Its energy is potent in overcoming sluggishness and restoring vitality.

Ruby is a detoxifier and stimulates the kidneys, adrenals, reproductive organs and spleen.

Care instructions:

Can overstimulate in sensitive people.

Tips for use in healing:

Work with Ruby to clear any energetic blockages, particularly in your root or heart chakra. Place your stone over the appropriate chakra, and breathe the warm, red energies into that area. As you breathe out, visualize the negativity leaving your body as black smoke.

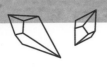

How did you work with Ruby?

....

....

How do you feel about the way you chose to work with the crystal, and was this effective for you?

....

....

What energies did you sense or feel when using this crystal?

....

....

....

....

How did the red colour of Ruby make you feel?

....

....

....

....

....

Did you feel the effect of Ruby's stimulating energies, and if so in what ways?

....

....

....

....

Did Ruby help you with any particular issues of the heart?

....

....

Did you feel Ruby clearing away any negative energy from your body or energy field?

....

....

How do you think Ruby can help you going forward in your practice?

....

....

....

....

Aquamarine

Appearance: Light blue
Healing properties: Brings inner peace and tranquillity; rejuvenating; brings courage and self-love
Vibe: Cool and soothing
Associated chakra: Throat

Evocative of paradise, this beautiful crystal has strong associations with the sea, and its water energy can bring rejuvenation and a sense of well-being. Aquamarine's soothing energy sweeps away stress, leaving a calm mind and a clean aura.

It clears the throat chakra, aiding communication and is an ideal stone for artists and performers or public speakers. Its gentleness makes it highly beneficial for sensitive people.

Aquamarine is useful for ailments involving the throat or thyroid and facilitates closure on all levels, guiding the soul toward higher consciousness.

Care instructions:

Fades in sunlight and susceptible to heat.

Tips for use in healing:

Place Aquamarine over any painful areas to soothe inflammation.

Working with Aquamarine on your throat or breastbone can encourage clear and positive communication with others. It can also connect you with your true self, leading to the development of courage, confidence and self-love.

How did you choose to work with Aquamarine?

....
....
....

How were you feeling before your session?

....
....
....

How did you feel after working with Aquamarine?

....
....
....

Did Aquamarine bring something to your attention for
resolution?

....
....
....
....

How has the colour of Aquamarine captured your imagination?

....

....

....

Did you feel a connection with water or the sea as you worked with this stone?

....

....

....

Did this stone help you to resolve any communication issues that you may be experiencing in your life?

....

....

....

Will you work with Aquamarine again, and if so, are there any specific things you wish to work on with it?

....

....

....

Emerald

Appearance: Green
Healing properties: Opens the heart chakra and promotes unconditional love; aids confidence; brings truth and wisdom
Vibe: Loving and romantic
Associated chakra: Heart

Emerald is a stone of successful and abundant love. It opens the heart to receiving all forms of affection, inspiring compassion, patience, loyalty and unconditional love in partnership and friendship.

Emerald was said to be the favourite of the goddess Venus and brings confidence as well as offering truth and wisdom.

A stone of good luck, it helps in overcoming misfortune and has a soothing effect on the wearer. Its pure green ray makes it highly beneficial for healing the heart chakra, and it aids regeneration and recovery, assisting with the healing of serious illnesses.

Care instructions:
Can trigger negative emotions if worn continuously.

Tips for use in healing:
Meditating with Emerald can help you to connect more deeply with your inner self.

Holding Emerald can quench your temper if you find yourself steaming up in a flammable situation.

Emerald under the pillow is alleged to help soothe feelings of jealousy, especially if it's related to your love life.

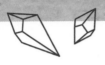

How did you choose to work with Emerald?

....

....

Did Emerald bring any heart-related issues to the surface for healing?

....

....

....

....

Draw your Emerald here:

Did Emerald share its wisdom, or reveal any inner truths to you?

....

....

....

....

Did working with Emerald help you connect more deeply with your inner self, and if so, how?

....

....

....

....

How did working with Emerald leave you feeling?

....

....

....

How would you like to work with this stone in the future?

....

....

....

Smoky Quartz

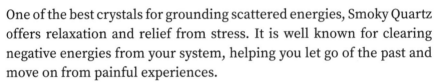

Appearance: Smoky brown, black or yellowish tint toward the end of a Clear Quartz. Artificially heated Smoky Quartz looks very black
Healing properties: Grounds scattered energies; energy cleanser that facilitates letting go
Vibe: Grounding, relaxing and supportive
Associated chakra: Root

One of the best crystals for grounding scattered energies, Smoky Quartz offers relaxation and relief from stress. It is well known for clearing negative energies from your system, helping you let go of the past and move on from painful experiences.

Always protective, it steels the nerves and allows anything no longer serving you, such as feelings of fear or depression, to leave your energy field, leaving you with a sense of peace. As well as eliminating emotional distress, it has detoxifying qualities that are useful for blocking electromagnetic stress.

Care instructions:

Quartz is fairly robust but should still be stored separately as it can be scratched by harder crystals such as Diamond, Topaz and Sapphire.

Tips for use in healing:

Tune in to your Smoky Quartz, and visualize it clearing away any negative energies that are hanging around in your energy field. You should feel lighter afterward.

Suggested affirmations to use with this stone include "I let go of anything that no longer serves me" or "I am grounded."

How did you choose to work with Smoky Quartz?

....

What effect did you feel its energies having on you?

....

....

....

Were you able to identify any negative energies present in your energy field, and what were they?

....

....

....

....

Describe the process of how the Smoky Quartz worked with you to clear negative energies, and how this made you feel.

....

....

....

....

Did you see any images while working with Smoky Quartz?

....

....

....

Has working with Smoky Quartz helped you to feel more connected to the earth?

....

Describe what your Smoky Quartz looks like in detail. Make notes on its texture, shape, fractures and colour.

....

....

....

....

Would you work with Smoky Quartz again, and if so, how do you intend to use this crystal in the future?

....

....

....

Jade

Appearance: Predominantly
green, but can also be blue,
cream, lavender, orange, red, brown
Healing properties: Brings good fortune
and abundance; longevity; wisdom
Vibe: Abundance, nurturing
Associated chakra: Heart

An extremely popular stone in China, Jade is known to sprinkle all areas of your life with prosperity and good luck. Work with Jade to access wisdom and allow it to bring harmony to your life; it supports your goals and brings new opportunities into your path. Its beautiful green rays stimulate the heart chakra, making it an excellent choice for nurturing and self-healing. Highly beneficial for the kidneys, Jade is wonderfully soothing and will help to release blocked emotions.

Allegedly it can help to tone down those wrinkles, as it's also associated with longevity, and is increasingly being utilized as a beauty aid.

Care instructions:

Chemicals such as chlorine can damage this stone so remove any Jade before entering a pool or hot tub.

Tips for use in healing:

Jade's smooth exterior means it's excellent as a "worry" stone. Stroke or rub it when you're feeling stressed or anxious.

Write down your goals for success – whether financial, career or healing-related. Place a thoroughly cleansed Jade stone on top of your list and ask it to guide you toward your desired achievements.

How did you choose to work with Jade? (e.g. manifestation, meditation)

....

Did you programme it to work with you in a specific way, or did you allow the crystal to bring the most appropriate thing to the surface for your awareness?

....

....

....

Did you think of areas where you would like to feel more abundance in your life?

....

....

....

....

Did Jade help you to identify some goals to work toward?

....

....

....

....

What did Jade bring to the surface for you that you were unaware of before?

....

....

....

How did you perceive Jade's energies and how did they make you feel?

....

....

....

....

Did Jade assist you to release any blocked energies or emotions?

....

....

....

How do you plan to work with Jade in the future?

....

....

....

Amber

Appearance: Orange, golden brown, yellow. Occasionally has insects or flora trapped inside
Healing properties: Transforms negative energy to positive; draws out disease
Vibe: Stimulating, positive and life-affirming
Associated chakras: Sacral, solar plexus

Amber is a powerful healer and protector, turning negative energies into positive ones and bringing disease to the surface for clearance. With strong connections to the earth, it helps the body to rebalance and heal itself by encouraging tissue revitalization.

Amber is a form of fossilized pine tree resin that is light in weight, yet it has the ability to absorb pain and bring vitality to the body.

Its vibrant colours can shift depression by cheering the wearer and creating a positive mental state. This makes it a good option for stress relief, and its sunny energies can stimulate the intellect and motivate the drive to achieve. It facilitates creative expression and offers wisdom, encouraging trust.

Care instructions:

Scratches easily. Avoid contact with perfume and don't cleanse Amber in water as it can damage the surface.

Tips for use in healing:

Amber absorbs pain and can be placed over any area for help with pain relief, whether physical or emotional.

Wear Amber in jewellery to transmute negative energies into positive ones.

How did you choose to use Amber?

....

Draw your Amber below:

Does your Amber have anything trapped inside it? If so, how has it changed the way you work with it?

....

....

....

How did you feel before using Amber?

....

....

....

How did you feel afterward?

....

....

....

Did Amber bring anything to the surface for clearance?

....

....

....

....

Did you use Amber for pain relief of any kind? If so, how did it help?

....

....

....

....

Garnet

Appearance: Brown, black, red, yellow, orange, green, pink
Healing properties: Grounding; good for matters of the heart; strengthening; stimulates energy flow
Vibe: Earthy
Associated chakras: All, depending on type

Strongly connected to earth and life-force energy, all Garnets have regenerative powers and can clear energy blockages and balance your *chi*. Garnet can help you to see your way out of tricky situations and is a good stone for matters of love – it can attract love and bring either harmony or passion depending on what the situation requires.

Working with Garnet can remove old patterns and release inhibitions. Types of Garnet include:

Red – love and heart energy; controls anger.

Brown (Almandine) – for strength and stamina. Facilitates energy flow between the root and crown chakras, promotes deep love.

Care instructions:

Garnet is fairly robust but should still be worn with care as it can get scratched.

Tips for use in healing:

Lying on a yoga mat (back flat to the floor) place Garnet between your feet and at the root and heart chakras. Ask for all seven chakras to be aligned. Visualize Garnet's energy spreading into your aura and breathe in its strengthening life-force energy.

When meditating with Garnet, breathe in positive universal energy and exhale any negativity blocking your energy flow. Work with an intention, such as to find balance or revive the passion in a long-term relationship. Sit quietly with the stone and allow it to wash away fears and anxieties.

How did you choose to work with Garnet?

....

Could you feel or sense Garnet's energies as they worked with you, and what did you feel?

....

....

....

Did you feel a strong connection to the earth as you worked with Garnet?

....

Did you ask Garnet to work with you in any particular area of your life?

....

....

....

If so, how did it help you in this area?

....

....

....

....

Did you see any images as you worked with Garnet?

....

....

....

Did you feel Garnet clearing any energy blockages, or releasing
any old patterns?

....

....

....

....

How did your energy flow alter after working with Garnet?

....

....

....

Will you work with Garnet again, and if so, in what way?

....

....

....

....

Rhodonite

Appearance: Pink or red. Marbled, with black veins
Healing properties: Teaches unconditional love, compassion and forgiveness in relationships
Vibe: Nurturing
Associated chakra: Heart

One of the most powerful heart chakra stones, Rhodonite is ideal for issues with relationships, helping to release toxic emotions. Working with Rhodonite helps break tendencies toward self-destruction and abusive or co-dependent relationships. It brings resentment or anger to the surface for clearance and encourages rational communication in order to move things forward.

Rhodonite clears the heart and encourages unconditional love, of both the self and others.

It teaches compassion and forgiveness and is especially useful when called upon to heal long-term abuse and trauma. The black veining sometimes present in Rhodonite can work to absorb any dark energies in the heart, while the pink energy vibrates unconditional love and compassion.

Care instructions:
Store Rhodonite separately to other crystals, as it can be scratched.

Tips for use in healing:
Hold Rhodonite over your heart to release negative emotions and enter a state of forgiveness.

Rhodonite heals physical as well as emotional wounds. Place on the skin to nurture external wounds.

If you're working with Rhodonite to find forgiveness in a particular situation, work with the following affirmation: "I forgive."

How did you choose to work with Rhodonite?

....

How did you connect with the pink energies of this stone and
how did they make you feel?

....

....

....

....

Did you feel any strong emotions such as anger, resentment or
frustration coming up for release?

....

....

....

....

Did your stone have any black veining within it, and did you feel
this working with you in a different yet complementary way to
the pink energy of your stone?

....

....

....

....

Did Rhodonite work with you to assist in letting go of a painful situation, and if so, how successful was this? (Some issues may take consistent and multiple sessions to resolve.)

....

....

....

....

Did Rhodonite teach you anything about compassion?

....

....

....

How do you feel Rhodonite has helped you to move forward?

....

....

....

Will you continue working with Rhodonite and if so how will you use it?

....

....

....

....

Lapis Lazuli

Appearance: Blue, marbled with white or threaded with gold
Healing properties: Pain and stress relief; assists self-expression
Vibe: Soothing
Associated chakras: Third eye, throat

This vivid electric blue stone is good for both pain and stress relief, leaving behind a deep sense of peace. It's suitable for easing migraines and other stress-related issues.

Working in the throat chakra, it reveals inner wisdom and encourages you to listen to and trust your own advice, so be prepared for a voyage to the heart of the authentic self. It also releases repressed anger and can help you to express yourself in an appropriate way.

If it's working in the third eye, Lapis Lazuli inspires creativity and dreams along with the development of your intuition and psychic abilities. Due to its peaceful properties, it's an aid for insomnia and can help to soothe emotional and physical suffering.

Care instructions:

A soft stone, it's susceptible to chipping and scratches. Avoid cleaning with soap and use cool or warm water only.

Tips for use in healing:

Wear at the throat for empowered and authentic self-expression, or place on the third eye to stimulate intuition and inner wisdom.

Lapis is a good stone for deepening your meditation practice. It can also be used as part of a healing grid with a Clear Quartz for amplification of intention, and protective Smoky Quartz in the lower part of the grid for grounding.

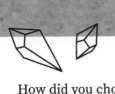

How did you choose to work with Lapis Lazuli?

....

....

Did Lapis reveal any insights or wisdoms to you?

....

....

....

....

What feelings did you experience working with its blue colour energy?

....

....

....

....

Did you work with Lapis on your third eye, and if so, did you receive any visions or images?

....

....

....

....

Did you use Lapis to relieve either pain or stress? If so, describe this process and whether it worked for you.

....

....

....

....

Did you use Lapis to work on any communication issues? If so, what?

....

....

Do you feel more connected to your inner or authentic self after working with Lapis? If so, how?

....

....

....

Do you feel more empowered after working with Lapis? If so, describe how its energies and wisdom have affected you.

....

....

....

....

Moonstone

Appearance: White, cream, yellow, green-blue. Often pearlescent or milky
Healing properties: Intuitive; good for female issues
Vibe: Soft, feminine, trippy
Associated chakras: Crown, third eye

This lovely sheeny stone works with the intuition of the third eye and has a soft feminine energy that's connected to the moon. This makes Moonstone ideal for supporting female issues such as hormone imbalance, menstruation and the reproductive cycle.

Moonstone has a nurturing energy that soothes emotions and can temper overreactions. It allows you to be reflective, reminding you that new beginnings are inevitable, because everything is subject to the cycles of nature and the constant flux of the universe. Moonstone can provide balance amidst the turbulence and remind you that the darkness of the night sky soon turns into light. Follow the guidance of the Moonstone as it lights up your path and guides you toward your purpose.

Care instructions:

Heat or sudden changes in temperature can cause fractures, so use warm (not hot) water to cleanse.

Tips for use in healing:

Place Moonstone over the solar plexus or heart to resolve negative emotional patterns.

If you're feeling lost or uncertain, hold Moonstone in your hand and tune in to it to reconnect with your purpose and find your path.

Align your Moonstone manifestation practice with the lunar cycle to give your manifestations extra potency. Programme your crystal with your intention, and the energy of the moon will amplify it. Moonstone is especially powerful around the full moon.

How did you choose to work with Moonstone?

....

Did you find yourself visualizing the moon or connecting to lunar energies while working with this stone?

....

....

....

How did this feel?

....

....

....

Did you experience visualizations of light and/or darkness while working with this stone? Describe any experiences you had with light energy or colours.

....

....

....

....

How did Moonstone guide you?

....

....

....

....

Did you see any images while working with Moonstone?

....

....

....

....

Did you work with your Moonstone during a particular phase of the lunar cycle, and if so which phase was it?

....

How did the wisdom you received from Moonstone tie in with that part of the lunar cycle?

....

....

....

Carnelian

Appearance: Red, orange, pink, brown
Healing properties: Boosts abundance;
passion; courage; self confidence
Vibe: Fiery and dynamic
Associated chakras: Root, sacral

Fiery Carnelian will ignite your creative spirit and is a great stone for artists as it enhances self-expression. It can bring vitality and passion in areas where you may have become stagnant and will motivate you to chase your wildest dreams once again, as it encourages bold action.

Carnelian teaches courage and confidence, energizing the lower three chakras, restoring strength while grounding your energy. It's also thought to bring abundance and sharpen concentration, paving the way for success. Carnelian protects against envy and resentment and soothes fiery tempers.

Care instructions:

Store Carnelian away from harder crystals to avoid scratching.

Tips for use in healing:

Meditate with Carnelian to unlock creativity and hit your full creative stride.

If you're feeling ungrounded or usually have trouble concentrating during meditation, Carnelian is ideal as it focuses the mind.

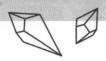

How did you choose to work with Carnelian? (e.g. meditation)

....

Did you ask it to work with you in a particular way, for example to help generate new creative ideas, overcome a creative block or to give you courage?

....

....

....

If so, how effective did you find Carnelian at helping with these issues?

....

....

....

....

....

How did you experience Carnelian energies?

....

....

....

Did you feel Carnelian working in any particular areas of your body?

....

....

....

....

What are your wildest (but realistic!) dreams?

....

....

....

....

....

Do you plan to work with Carnelian to help you achieve them, and if so how?

....

....

....

....

....

Agate

Appearance: Pink, brown, blue, green, milky white, grey, clear, banded. Sometimes artificially coloured
Healing properties: Strengthens; reveals inner truths; dissolves inner conflict; promotes balance and self-acceptance
Vibe: Stabilizing, grounding
Associated chakras: All, depending on type

Agates can be found in many different types and colours, but the bands that run around the stone are a specific Agate feature that relate to its multiple layers of formation. These layers work with the compound layers within yourself, peeling back deposits of emotion or bringing hidden truths to light, guiding you toward resolution of internal conflict. Agate works slowly but brings great strength and encourages the wearer to speak their truth, and to practise self-acceptance and self-awareness. It helps dissolve inner anger, foster love and provide the courage to start over.

Emotionally calming and balancing, its grounding properties can help improve concentration. Some Agates, such as Botswana, Moss or Blue Lace, have additional properties on top of the more generalized ones above.

Care instructions:

Never use household chemicals to clean Agate. Store it separately from other stones to avoid scratching.

Tips for use in healing:

Spend time in quiet contemplation with Agate to nurture spiritual growth and inner stability.

Place Agate over the heart to release any blockages preventing the acceptance of love.

Place Agate on the stomach to relieve gastritis or other digestive issues, as it stimulates digestion.

How did you choose to work with Agate?

....

What type is your Agate? (e.g. traditional banded, as described above, or a specialized type such as Moss Agate)

....

Draw your Agate below:

What emotions did you feel when working with Agate?

....

....

....

Did Agate bring any truths to the surface or any internal conflict for resolution?

....

....

....

....

Did Agate help you to become aware of anything that you were not previously aware of about yourself?

....

....

....

How did you feel after your practice with Agate?

....

....

....

....

Clear Quartz

Appearance: Clear
Healing properties: Useful for mental clarity and major life path decisions; powerful healer, good for any issue or illness
Vibe: Clarifying
Associated chakras: All

Clear Quartz is a must-have in every crystal collection. It's known as a master healer because of its powerful amplifying and healing abilities. It can offer help for every issue and disorder as it contains every colour.

Just like its crystal-clear appearance, it helps with mental clarity and focusing thought, so it can help you to decide on what you really want in life. It's great if you're studying for exams as it aids concentration and helps to unlock memory.

Care instructions:

Don't leave Clear Quartz out on a flammable surface, as it acts like a magnifying glass in sunlight and could start a fire.

Tips for use in healing:

Use Clear Quartz in a grid or with other stones if you want to amplify healing or manifestation.

Because of its ability to amplify intentions, Clear Quartz is an excellent stone for manifestation. If you find yourself having to make a difficult decision, ask Clear Quartz to help you see the way forward.

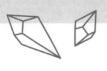

How did you work with Clear Quartz?

....

....

Do you have any major life decisions coming up that you need guidance with? If so, what are they?

....

....

....

....

....

Did you work with Clear Quartz on these, and if so how did it help?

....

....

....

....

How did you experience Clear Quartz's energies?

....

....

....

Did you work with Clear Quartz to heal any physical or emotional issues, and if so, which?

....

....

....

Describe how your Clear Quartz was able to assist with these issues.

....

....

....

....

Will you work with Clear Quartz again? If so, will you work with it as a healer or amplifier of manifestation or both?

....

List some other life choices, or any outstanding issues you didn't work on in this session, that Clear Quartz could potentially help you with next time:

....

....

....

....

Snowflake Obsidian

Appearance: Black with white snowflake-type spots
Healing properties: Brings buried truths to the surface for clearing
Vibe: Balancing, soothing
Associated chakra: Root

This beautiful stone looks as if snowflakes have settled on it and has the same soothing effect as watching snowflakes gently fall and settle outside.

As Obsidian is a shadow stone (meaning it works on the things that are lurking in your subconscious), it will bring up ingrained mental and behavioural patterns for release, which may be initially uncomfortable for some. Of all the Obsidian stones, the Snowflake variety is the gentlest and can teach you to appreciate your mistakes as much as your successes.

Snowflake Obsidian is balancing and purifying and can help you to reframe isolation and loneliness so they become a superpower rather than a restriction.

Care instructions:

Snowflake Obsidian can be brittle and should not be cleansed with any household chemicals.

Tips for use in healing:

Use Snowflake Obsidian in meditation to aid surrender.
Place on the sacral chakra to instil a sense of calm.

How did you work with Snowflake Obsidian?

....

Is the energy of this stone different from the other crystals you
have worked with, and if so, how?

....

....

....

Draw your Snowflake Obsidian here:

Did Snowflake Obsidian bring any hidden truths to the surface for release? If so, which?

....

....

....

....

....

Did these truths take you by surprise? If so, why?

....

....

....

Did Snowflake Obsidian highlight any mental or behavioural patterns for release? If so, which?

....

....

....

How did you find working with Snowflake Obsidian?

....

....

....

Sunstone

Appearance: Orange, gold, red-brown
Healing properties: Lifts mood
Vibe: Joyful and sunny
Associated chakras: Solar plexus, sacral

Life is sweet with Sunstone shining on you. This is the perfect crystal to raise low mood, filling your energy field with its sunny rays and dissipating those cloudy feelings, leaving you full of joy and confidence instead. Sunstone wants you to shine and be your best self, so no wonder it is often linked to good fortune.

It will take you for a walk on the bright side of life and remind you to enjoy every moment, big or small. Its optimism and connection with the healing power of the sun can bring deep emotional healing.

Care instructions:

Sunstone can be scratched if it comes into contact with harder crystals, so store separately.

Tips for use in healing:

Meditate with Sunstone for joy and happiness, or to connect with your inner light.

Sunstone loves to be charged in the sun, and if you're able to meditate with it outside this enhances its effect.

For chakra cleansing, place Sunstone on the throat for loving communication, on the solar plexus to help lift repressed, heavy or stagnant emotions, or on the sacral chakra to stimulate passion and creativity.

How did you work with Sunstone? (e.g. meditation, or chakra cleansing)

....

....

How did you feel before your session with Sunstone?

....

....

....

....

How did you feel afterward?

....

....

....

....

Name three areas where you could improve confidence or joy in your life:

....

....

....

Did Sunstone touch on any areas where you could improve confidence or joy in your life? Or is this something you may work on in the future with Sunstone?

....

....

....

Did you see any colours in your mind's eye when you were working with Sunstone?

....

....

Did you feel the sun energy of Sunstone, and has it helped you to feel more optimistic about your current life situation or the future? If so, how?

....

....

....

Has Sunstone helped you to feel more confident or optimistic in yourself? If so, how?

....

....

....

Aventurine

Appearance: Green, red, peach, blue, brown, with sparkly flecks
Healing properties:
Brings fortune and prosperity; heart healer
Vibe: Lucky
Associated chakra: Heart

Known as one of the luckiest stones, take Aventurine with you to that job interview or on a promising first date. If you work with its belief that you create your own luck with a positive attitude, it will sprinkle its glitter over all areas of your life.

Aventurine opens and works with the heart centre, encouraging compassion and perseverance, and teaches you to see possibility in every situation. It teaches that luck is a mindset and helps you remove doubts and negativity so that you're in the correct energetic place to attract and recognize new opportunities. Aventurine's confidence also helps with leadership and making decisions.

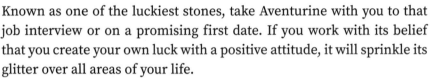

Care instructions:
Fades in sunlight.

Tips for use in healing:
Carry Aventurine with you or wear it as a lucky charm.

If you're feeling down on your luck, hold Aventurine in your hand and visualize it clearing all the negative energy in your mind and energy field. Feel it connecting you into the flow of abundance, luck and prosperity.

How did you choose to work with Aventurine?

....

In what areas of life are you looking to create luck and
opportunity?

....

....

....

....

....

Did you work with Aventurine on any of these areas today?

....

....

....

....

Did Aventurine help you with any heart-related emotions or
issues? If so, which?

....

....

....

....

What were your experiences of working with Aventurine? Did you feel anything happen in your heart area, or a sense of optimism fill your energy field?

....

....

....

....

....

Did you see any colours or images while working with Aventurine, or feel any sensations on your body or in your energy field?

....

....

....

....

Did you like working with Aventurine, and will you work with it in the future? If so, how will you work with it in your next healing session?

....

....

....

....

Calcite

Appearance: Blue, green, orange, yellow, clear, brown, pink (mangano), red
Healing properties: Relieves stress; encourages creativity and motivation; hastens spiritual growth
Vibe: Chilled, supportive and stabilizing
Associated chakras: All, depending on colour

Calcite is good at eliminating stagnant energy and relieving stress, replacing it with tranquillity and leaving you feeling lighter. An encouraging support stone, it can help those lacking in hope or motivation and is said to convert ideas into action. Calcite soothes the mind and sharpens insight. It's a great warrior to have by your side to vanquish setbacks. A stabilizing stone, it accelerates gentle spiritual growth and encourages you to trust in yourself.

Of the many different types of Calcite, one of the most popular is Green Calcite, a calming energy cleanser with green heart and earth energy. It restores mental balance and facilitates letting go. Orange Calcite is a joyful, energizing stone, perfect for work on the lower chakras.

Care instructions:

Scratches easily. Take care with light-coloured Calcites, such as blue or green, as they fade in sunlight and may prefer being kept somewhere dark.

Tips for use in healing:

Meditate with an Orange Calcite in the sacral chakra to help unblock creativity.

Place a Blue Calcite on the throat chakra if you're preparing to communicate clearly about something.

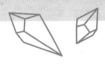

Which colour of Calcite did you work with?

....

....

How did you feel you responded to the Calcite's energies? What effect did they have on you?

....

....

....

....

....

....

Did working with Calcite provide you with any insight?

....

....

....

....

....

....

....

Has Calcite motivated you to turn any ideas into action and if so, which ones?

....

....

....

....

....

What energies did Calcite help you to clear, if any?

....

....

....

....

Will you work with Calcite again, and will you work with other colours or the same Calcite?

....

What spiritual goals can Calcite assist you to work toward next time?

....

....

....

....

Tiger's Eye

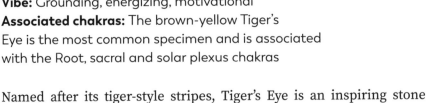

Appearance: Brown-yellow,
red, pink, blue. Banded
Healing properties: Instils
courage and dissipates fear
Vibe: Grounding, energizing, motivational
Associated chakras: The brown-yellow Tiger's
Eye is the most common specimen and is associated
with the Root, sacral and solar plexus chakras

Named after its tiger-style stripes, Tiger's Eye is an inspiring stone that encourages you to step into your own power. It carries both earth and sun energy, meaning it combines a strong grounding energy with aspirational energy.

It works particularly well with the solar plexus, helping you to develop the courage and confidence to accomplish your goals and healing any self-esteem issues. It can help silence your inner critic, while showing you any faults, obstacles or belief systems that need to be overcome.

Tiger's Eye encourages you to grab life by the horns: to feel the fear and do it anyway.

Care Instructions:

Tiger's Eye is a durable stone but best stored separately to prevent scratching from other crystals.

Tips for use in healing:

Carry a Tiger's Eye for courage. Whenever you find yourself in a situation that requires a boost of confidence, stroke your crystal and connect with its energy.

Meditate with Tiger's Eye on the lower chakras, where it can ground scattered energies.

How did you choose to use Tiger's Eye?

....

Draw a picture of your Tiger's Eye below:

Were there any goals you asked Tiger's Eye to help you with?

....

....

....

....

Are there any areas in your life where you could use more confidence? Did you ask for Tiger's Eye's assistance with these?

....

....

....

....

How did you respond to the energies of Tiger's Eye, and how did you feel them working in your body or energy field?

....

....

....

....

How did you feel after working with Tiger's Eye?

....

....

....

Has this stone unlocked any barriers for you and given you a way to move forward?

....

....

....

Kyanite

Appearance: Blue-white,
black, grey, green
Healing properties: Throat and
voice; assists in speaking your truth
Vibe: Spiritual
Associated chakra: Throat

This high vibration, spiritual crystal is known to stabilize and replenish the physical body, while enhancing your connection with spirit guides and spiritual truth. Said to promote healing dreams, it also works with the throat chakra to clear any communication issues and help you speak your truth. It shows the individual the part they are playing in the course of their own life, rather than simply putting things down to fate or karma.

The most common varieties of Kyanite are found in blue-white and black. Blue Kyanite is especially effective with the throat chakra and voice, and a good stone for performers. Black Kyanite is a lovely grounding stone that helps you to cut ties with any toxic people who are draining your energy.

Care instructions:
Kyanite is fragile and breaks easily.

Tips for use in healing:
With its high vibrations and connection to the spiritual realm, Kyanite is a wonderful stone for meditation. Meditate with Kyanite to connect with your spirit guides.

Hold Black Kyanite in your hand as you visualize neutralizing and protecting yourself against negative attachments.

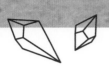

How did you choose to work with Kyanite?

....

Which colour of Kyanite did you work with?

....

Did Kyanite help you with any communication issues you have been struggling with? If so, what where they, and how did it help you?

....

....

....

....

....

Did Kyanite help you to uncover any truths about yourself, or deeper spiritual truths?

....

....

....

....

....

Did you connect with any spirit guides while working with Kyanite? Explain who you connected with and what you saw or learned.

....

....

....

....

....

Did you see any other visions or images while working with Kyanite?

....

....

....

....

What effect did Kyanite have on you energetically?

....

How did you feel after working with Kyanite?

....

....

....

Black Tourmaline

Appearance: Black
Healing properties: Absorbs and cleanses negative energy
Vibe: Grounding, protective
Associated chakra: Root

Another must-have for any crystal collection, the deeply protective Black Tourmaline is a lovely stone to wear and have in your home. An all-round energy cleanser, it will keep negative energies away from you and, when placed by the front door, out of your home. It also helps to absorb electromagnetic and other environmental pollution, so it's a good stone to place near electronic goods.

Black Tourmaline is a very grounding stone, filling the space that negative energies previously occupied with positive, life-force energy. It encourages rational thinking and a constructive attitude in any situation.

Care instructions:

Susceptible to flaking. Handle carefully and do not cleanse in water. Store separately.

Tips for use in healing:

Use Black Tourmaline in daily cleansing rituals. Hold the stone in your left hand and visualize its rays entering your energy field. Imagine it purifying any negative energy and eliminating it from your aura.

Remember to cleanse Black Tourmaline regularly, as it absorbs negative energy like a sponge.

How did you choose to work with Black Tourmaline?

....

....

Did you sense Black Tourmaline's energies? What did you feel?

....

....

....

....

....

....

Did the crystal work to remove any negative energies and if so, do you know what they were?

....

....

....

....

....

....

....

How did you feel before you worked with Black Tourmaline?

....

....

....

....

How did you feel after your session with Black Tourmaline?

....

....

....

....

Did you experience any visualizations or images with this stone?

....

....

....

....

How might you use Black Tourmaline in the future?

....

....

Bloodstone

Appearance: Green with flecks of red
Healing properties: Good health; revitalizes the mind, body, spirit
Vibe: Stimulating
Associated chakras: Root, heart

Revitalizing Bloodstone can get both the physical and creative juices flowing again when the body and mind are exhausted. Known as a blood cleanser and immune-system stimulator, it's a good stone to work with for overall health and vitality.

It also has grounding and protective properties, while its dynamism propels you out of mental paralysis to be able to live in the present moment with courage. It clears and focuses the mind, heightening intuition and creativity.

Bloodstone grounds heart energy, while its zest for life will help you to push through any challenges.

Care instructions:

Don't wear Bloodstone when exercising or cleaning, to avoid scratching, and keep it away from chemicals or extreme temperatures. Store separately to avoid scratching.

Tips for use in healing:

Meditate with Bloodstone to stimulate the root chakra and blast away sluggishness from your system.

Try a walking meditation to stimulate the blood flow and any stagnant energy. Create a quiet and clutter-free space and light some incense if desired. Hold Bloodstone in your hand and focus on putting one foot in front of the other in slow pigeon steps until you are concentrating in the moment on your physical activity. Feel the life-force energy flow through your body with each step.

How did you choose to work with Bloodstone?

....

....

Are there any challenges that you've been facing recently?

....

....

....

....

....

Did you ask Bloodstone to assist you with the courage and energy to tackle the challenges listed above?

....

....

Did Bloodstone's energies have a physical effect on your body?

....

....

....

....

....

How did you feel before you worked with Bloodstone?

....

....

....

....

....

....

How did you feel afterward?

....

....

....

....

Will you work with Bloodstone again and if so, how?

....

....

....

....

....

....

Malachite

Appearance: Green, banded
Healing properties: Transformative;
removes negative patterning
Vibe: Psychedelic, trippy, but earthy
Associated chakras: Heart, third eye

Known as a stone of transformation, Malachite is an appropriate stone for our times. If change is needed in any area of your life, you can be sure Malachite will sniff it out and help you to take the leap. Malachite will bring anything preventing your growth to the surface, pruning out anything that's no longer needed and opening the heart to unconditional love.

With its hallucinogenic-looking patterns, it can trigger images, dreams and connection to other realms, while also being a stone that is deeply connected to nature and regeneration.

It soaks up negative energies and pollutants readily and should be cleansed often.

Care instructions:

Don't cleanse Malachite in salt, as it will damage the surface. Malachite is toxic and should only be used as a polished stone.

Tips for use in healing:

Use on the solar plexus to dissolve negative emotions.

Meditate with Malachite on the third eye for a deep dive into the realm of nature spirits and earth intelligence.

How did you choose to work with Malachite?

....

Draw your Malachite below:

When you look at your Malachite crystal, what response does it elicit in you?

....

....

....

....

Did you see any images while working with Malachite?

....
....
....
....

Did you feel connected with nature when working with
Malachite?

....
....
....
....

Did Malachite bring up any emotional, mental or behavioural
patterns for removal?

....
....
....

Will you work with Malachite again, and if so how?

....
....
....

Haematite

Appearance: Silver-grey, black, red
Healing properties: Balancing;
strengthening; dissolves negative energies
Vibe: Grounding, fortifying
Associated chakra: Root

Haematite has a strong grounding and strengthening energy, which comes naturally from its iron composition.

Its energy protects your aura, preventing negative energies from entering by dissolving them and balancing the mind, body and spirit. It can offer a feeling of security and allow the body and mind to realign into a peaceful state.

Haematite can boost confidence, particularly in women, and is useful for relief from insomnia caused by a scattered mind. Haematite can help you to see past mistakes as learning experiences.

Care instructions:

Avoid contact with chlorine or cleansing in salt or water. Haematite contains iron oxide, so rusts easily.

Tips for use in healing:

Use for any blood-related issues.

Ground and balance both sides of the body by holding a Haematite in each hand.

Meditating with this stone can connect you with your inner strength.

Hold Haematite or wear as a bracelet and tune in to its energies if you're feeling insecure or need to stand your ground in a stressful situation.

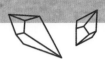

How did you choose to work with Haematite?

....

....

How did you experience Haematite's energies?

....

....

....

....

....

How did you feel before working with Haematite?

....

....

....

....

How did you feel after working with Haematite?

....

....

....

....

Did Haematite bring anything up for resolution, or bring anything to your awareness?

....

....

....

....

....

Did you feel more connected to your inner strength working with Haematite?

....

....

....

....

Will you work with Haematite again, and if so, how?

....

....

....

....

....

....

Charoite

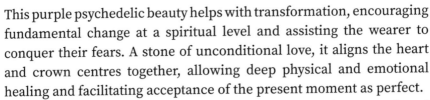

Appearance: Purple. Patterned
with veins or spirals
Healing properties: Conquering
fear; accepting change
Vibe: Relaxing, transformative and deeply healing
Associated chakras: Heart, third eye, crown

This purple psychedelic beauty helps with transformation, encouraging fundamental change at a spiritual level and assisting the wearer to conquer their fears. A stone of unconditional love, it aligns the heart and crown centres together, allowing deep physical and emotional healing and facilitating acceptance of the present moment as perfect.

This chilled-out stone can help you to relax when you're stressed, and you can work with it to overcome obsessions and other compulsions.

Said to be able to convert disease into wellness, this vibrant stone can help relieve insomnia and induce vivid dreams.

Care instructions:

Sensitive to heat.

Tips for use in healing:

Work with Charoite to open and balance your crown chakra. Lie down in a comfortable position and place your Charoite at the crown of your head. Visualize a purple or white light coming through the crystal, shining into and filling your crown energy centre. Imagine the light cleansing away any blockages or negativity. If you are experiencing feelings of alienation or frustration, ask the Charoite specifically to help with this, or simply allow the stone to open, heal, cleanse, balance and align your chakra. Allow the stone to work until you feel a sense of peace or calm.

How did you work with Charoite?

....

Draw a picture of your crystal here:

Are there any major changes you're going through in life at the moment?

....

....

....

....

Did Charoite assist you in any way with any feelings or emotions around these changes?

....

....

....

....

How did you connect with Charoite's energies?

....

....

....

Did Charoite bring any fears to the surface for release?

....

....

....

Do you intend to work with Charoite again, and if so, in what way will you work with it next time?

....

....

....

MY
HEALING
JOURNAL

Crystal: ....

Colour, shape, texture and any other notable features:

....

....

....

....

Drawing of your crystal:

Did you programme the crystal or ask it to work in a certain way with you?

....

....

Did you experience any sensations or feelings while working with your crystal?

....

....

....

Did you see any images while using your crystal?

....

....

....

....

....

Did the crystal give you a message?

....

....

....

Did the crystal bring any issues to the surface for resolution?

....

....

....

....

Did you feel the crystal working in a particular area of your body?

....

Is there any follow-up work needed on any issues brought to light?
What did the crystal teach you about yourself?

....

....

Crystal: ....

Colour, shape, texture and any other notable features:

....

....

....

....

Drawing of your crystal:

Did you programme the crystal or ask it to work in a certain way
with you?

....

....

Did you experience any sensations or feelings while working with
your crystal?

....

....

....

Did you see any images while using your crystal?

....

....

....

....

....

Did the crystal give you a message?

....

....

....

Did the crystal bring any issues to the surface for resolution?

....

....

....

....

Did you feel the crystal working in a particular area of your body?

....

Is there any follow-up work needed on any issues brought to light?
What did the crystal teach you about yourself?

....

....

Crystal: ....

Colour, shape, texture and any other notable features:

....

....

....

....

Drawing of your crystal:

Did you programme the crystal or ask it to work in a certain way with you?

....

....

Did you experience any sensations or feelings while working with your crystal?

....

....

....

Did you see any images while using your crystal?

....

....

....

....

....

Did the crystal give you a message?

....

....

....

Did the crystal bring any issues to the surface for resolution?

....

....

....

....

Did you feel the crystal working in a particular area of your body?

....

Is there any follow-up work needed on any issues brought to light?
What did the crystal teach you about yourself?

....

....

Crystal: ....

Colour, shape, texture and any other notable features:

....

....

....

....

Drawing of your crystal:

Did you programme the crystal or ask it to work in a certain way with you?

....

....

Did you experience any sensations or feelings while working with your crystal?

....

....

....

Did you see any images while using your crystal?

....

....

....

....

....

Did the crystal give you a message?

....

....

....

Did the crystal bring any issues to the surface for resolution?

....

....

....

....

Did you feel the crystal working in a particular area of your body?

....

Is there any follow-up work needed on any issues brought to light? What did the crystal teach you about yourself?

....

....

Crystal: ....

Colour, shape, texture and any other notable features:

....

....

....

....

Drawing of your crystal:

Did you programme the crystal or ask it to work in a certain way with you?

....

....

Did you experience any sensations or feelings while working with your crystal?

....

....

....

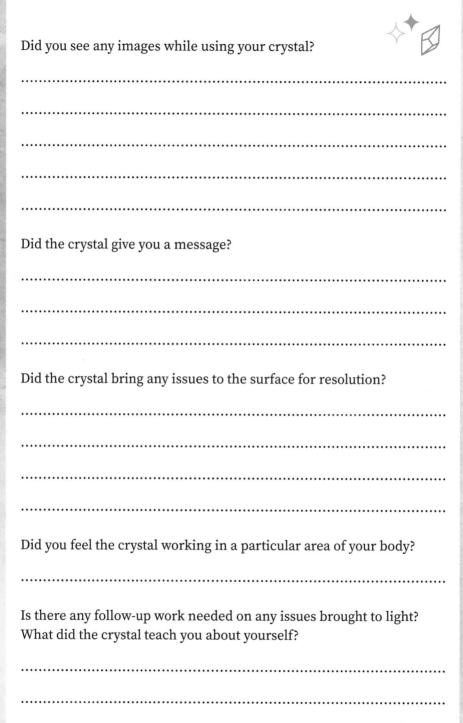

Did you see any images while using your crystal?

....

....

....

....

....

Did the crystal give you a message?

....

....

....

Did the crystal bring any issues to the surface for resolution?

....

....

....

....

Did you feel the crystal working in a particular area of your body?

....

Is there any follow-up work needed on any issues brought to light?
What did the crystal teach you about yourself?

....

....

Crystal: ....

Colour, shape, texture and any other notable features:

....

....

....

....

Drawing of your crystal:

Did you programme the crystal or ask it to work in a certain way
with you?

....

....

Did you experience any sensations or feelings while working with
your crystal?

....

....

....

Did you see any images while using your crystal?

....

....

....

....

....

Did the crystal give you a message?

....

....

....

Did the crystal bring any issues to the surface for resolution?

....

....

....

....

Did you feel the crystal working in a particular area of your body?

....

Is there any follow-up work needed on any issues brought to light?
What did the crystal teach you about yourself?

....

....

Crystal: ....

Colour, shape, texture and any other notable features:

....

....

....

....

Drawing of your crystal:

Did you programme the crystal or ask it to work in a certain way with you?

....

....

Did you experience any sensations or feelings while working with your crystal?

....

....

....

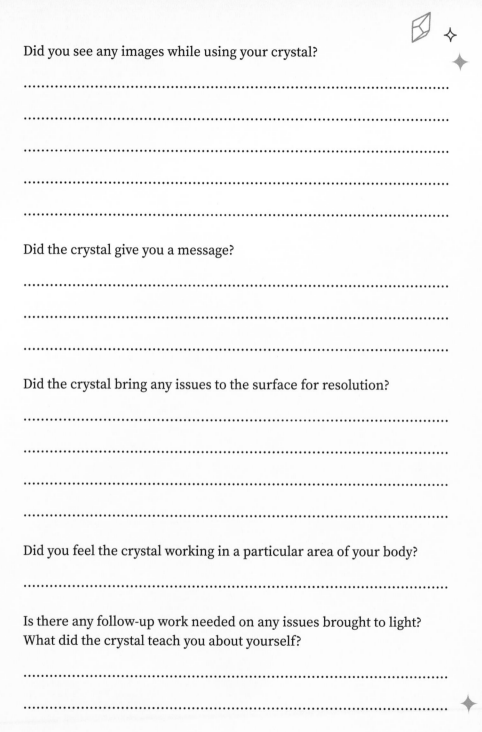

Did you see any images while using your crystal?

....

....

....

....

....

Did the crystal give you a message?

....

....

....

Did the crystal bring any issues to the surface for resolution?

....

....

....

....

Did you feel the crystal working in a particular area of your body?

....

Is there any follow-up work needed on any issues brought to light?
What did the crystal teach you about yourself?

....

....

Crystal: ....

Colour, shape, texture and any other notable features:

....

....

....

....

Drawing of your crystal:

Did you programme the crystal or ask it to work in a certain way with you?

....

....

Did you experience any sensations or feelings while working with your crystal?

....

....

....

Did you see any images while using your crystal?

....

....

....

....

....

Did the crystal give you a message?

....

....

....

Did the crystal bring any issues to the surface for resolution?

....

....

....

....

Did you feel the crystal working in a particular area of your body?

....

Is there any follow-up work needed on any issues brought to light?
What did the crystal teach you about yourself?

....

....

Crystal: ....

Colour, shape, texture and any other notable features:

....

....

....

....

Drawing of your crystal:

Did you programme the crystal or ask it to work in a certain way with you?

....

....

Did you experience any sensations or feelings while working with your crystal?

....

....

....

Did you see any images while using your crystal?

....

....

....

....

....

Did the crystal give you a message?

....

....

....

Did the crystal bring any issues to the surface for resolution?

....

....

....

....

Did you feel the crystal working in a particular area of your body?

....

Is there any follow-up work needed on any issues brought to light?
What did the crystal teach you about yourself?

....

....

Crystal: ....

Colour, shape, texture and any other notable features:

....

....

....

....

Drawing of your crystal:

Did you programme the crystal or ask it to work in a certain way with you?

....

....

Did you experience any sensations or feelings while working with your crystal?

....

....

....

Did you see any images while using your crystal?

....

....

....

....

....

Did the crystal give you a message?

....

....

....

Did the crystal bring any issues to the surface for resolution?

....

....

....

....

Did you feel the crystal working in a particular area of your body?

....

Is there any follow-up work needed on any issues brought to light?
What did the crystal teach you about yourself?

....

....

Crystal: ....

Colour, shape, texture and any other notable features:

....

....

....

....

Drawing of your crystal:

Did you programme the crystal or ask it to work in a certain way with you?

....

....

Did you experience any sensations or feelings while working with your crystal?

....

....

....

Did you see any images while using your crystal?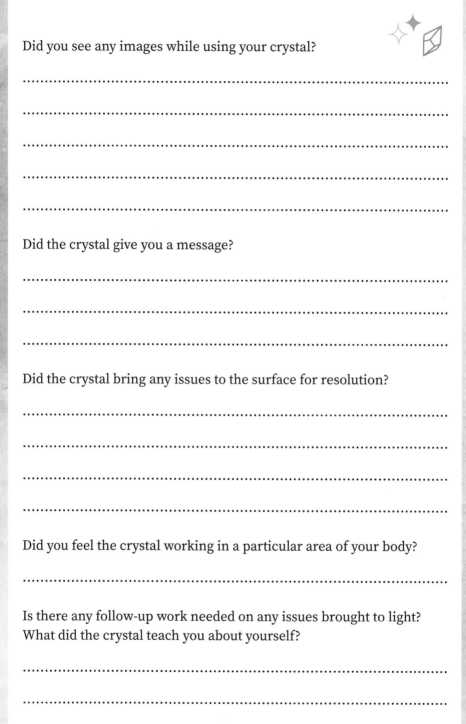

....

....

....

....

....

Did the crystal give you a message?

....

....

....

Did the crystal bring any issues to the surface for resolution?

....

....

....

....

Did you feel the crystal working in a particular area of your body?

....

Is there any follow-up work needed on any issues brought to light? What did the crystal teach you about yourself?

....

....

Crystal: ....

Colour, shape, texture and any other notable features:

....

....

....

....

Drawing of your crystal:

Did you programme the crystal or ask it to work in a certain way with you?

....

....

Did you experience any sensations or feelings while working with your crystal?

....

....

....

Did you see any images while using your crystal?

....

....

....

....

....

Did the crystal give you a message?

....

....

....

Did the crystal bring any issues to the surface for resolution?

....

....

....

....

Did you feel the crystal working in a particular area of your body?

....

Is there any follow-up work needed on any issues brought to light?
What did the crystal teach you about yourself?

....

....

Crystal: ....

Colour, shape, texture and any other notable features:

....
....
....
....

Drawing of your crystal:

Did you programme the crystal or ask it to work in a certain way with you?

....
....

Did you experience any sensations or feelings while working with your crystal?

....
....
....

Did you see any images while using your crystal?

....

....

....

....

....

Did the crystal give you a message?

....

....

....

Did the crystal bring any issues to the surface for resolution?

....

....

....

....

Did you feel the crystal working in a particular area of your body?

....

Is there any follow-up work needed on any issues brought to light?
What did the crystal teach you about yourself?

....

....

Crystal: ....

Colour, shape, texture and any other notable features:

....
....
....
....

Drawing of your crystal:

Did you programme the crystal or ask it to work in a certain way with you?

....
....

Did you experience any sensations or feelings while working with your crystal?

....
....
....

Did you see any images while using your crystal?

....

....

....

....

....

Did the crystal give you a message?

....

....

....

Did the crystal bring any issues to the surface for resolution?

....

....

....

....

Did you feel the crystal working in a particular area of your body?

....

Is there any follow-up work needed on any issues brought to light?
What did the crystal teach you about yourself?

....

....

Crystal: ....

Colour, shape, texture and any other notable features:

....
....
....
....

Drawing of your crystal:

Did you programme the crystal or ask it to work in a certain way with you?

....
....

Did you experience any sensations or feelings while working with your crystal?

....
....
....

Did you see any images while using your crystal?

....

....

....

....

....

Did the crystal give you a message?

....

....

....

Did the crystal bring any issues to the surface for resolution?

....

....

....

....

Did you feel the crystal working in a particular area of your body?

....

Is there any follow-up work needed on any issues brought to light?
What did the crystal teach you about yourself?

....

....

Crystal: ....

Colour, shape, texture and any other notable features:

....

....

....

....

Drawing of your crystal:

Did you programme the crystal or ask it to work in a certain way with you?

....

....

Did you experience any sensations or feelings while working with your crystal?

....

....

....

Did you see any images while using your crystal?

....

....

....

....

....

Did the crystal give you a message?

....

....

....

Did the crystal bring any issues to the surface for resolution?

....

....

....

....

Did you feel the crystal working in a particular area of your body?

....

Is there any follow-up work needed on any issues brought to light?
What did the crystal teach you about yourself?

....

....

Crystal: ....

Colour, shape, texture and any other notable features:

....

....

....

....

Drawing of your crystal:

Did you programme the crystal or ask it to work in a certain way
with you?

....

....

Did you experience any sensations or feelings while working with
your crystal?

....

....

....

Did you see any images while using your crystal?

....

....

....

....

....

Did the crystal give you a message?

....

....

....

Did the crystal bring any issues to the surface for resolution?

....

....

....

....

Did you feel the crystal working in a particular area of your body?

....

Is there any follow-up work needed on any issues brought to light? What did the crystal teach you about yourself?

....

....

Crystal: ....

Colour, shape, texture and any other notable features:

....

....

....

....

Drawing of your crystal:

Did you programme the crystal or ask it to work in a certain way with you?

....

....

Did you experience any sensations or feelings while working with your crystal?

....

....

....

Did you see any images while using your crystal?

....

....

....

....

....

Did the crystal give you a message?

....

....

....

Did the crystal bring any issues to the surface for resolution?

....

....

....

....

Did you feel the crystal working in a particular area of your body?

....

Is there any follow-up work needed on any issues brought to light? What did the crystal teach you about yourself?

....

....

Crystal: ....

Colour, shape, texture and any other notable features:

....

....

....

....

Drawing of your crystal:

Did you programme the crystal or ask it to work in a certain way with you?

....

....

Did you experience any sensations or feelings while working with your crystal?

....

....

....

Did you see any images while using your crystal?

....

....

....

....

....

Did the crystal give you a message?

....

....

....

Did the crystal bring any issues to the surface for resolution?

....

....

....

....

Did you feel the crystal working in a particular area of your body?

....

Is there any follow-up work needed on any issues brought to light?
What did the crystal teach you about yourself?

....

....

Crystal: ....

Colour, shape, texture and any other notable features:

....

....

....

....

Drawing of your crystal:

Did you programme the crystal or ask it to work in a certain way with you?

....

....

Did you experience any sensations or feelings while working with your crystal?

....

....

....

Did you see any images while using your crystal?

....

....

....

....

....

Did the crystal give you a message?

....

....

....

Did the crystal bring any issues to the surface for resolution?

....

....

....

....

Did you feel the crystal working in a particular area of your body?

....

Is there any follow-up work needed on any issues brought to light? What did the crystal teach you about yourself?

....

....

Crystal: ....

Colour, shape, texture and any other notable features:

....

....

....

....

Drawing of your crystal:

Did you programme the crystal or ask it to work in a certain way with you?

....

....

Did you experience any sensations or feelings while working with your crystal?

....

....

....

Did you see any images while using your crystal?

....

....

....

....

....

Did the crystal give you a message?

....

....

....

Did the crystal bring any issues to the surface for resolution?

....

....

....

....

Did you feel the crystal working in a particular area of your body?

....

Is there any follow-up work needed on any issues brought to light?
What did the crystal teach you about yourself?

....

....

Crystal: ....

Colour, shape, texture and any other notable features:

....

....

....

....

Drawing of your crystal:

Did you programme the crystal or ask it to work in a certain way with you?

....

....

Did you experience any sensations or feelings while working with your crystal?

....

....

....

Did you see any images while using your crystal?

....

....

....

....

....

Did the crystal give you a message?

....

....

....

Did the crystal bring any issues to the surface for resolution?

....

....

....

....

Did you feel the crystal working in a particular area of your body?

....

Is there any follow-up work needed on any issues brought to light?
What did the crystal teach you about yourself?

....

....

Crystal: ....

Colour, shape, texture and any other notable features:

....

....

....

....

Drawing of your crystal:

Did you programme the crystal or ask it to work in a certain way with you?

....

....

Did you experience any sensations or feelings while working with your crystal?

....

....

....

Did you see any images while using your crystal?

....

....

....

....

....

Did the crystal give you a message?

....

....

....

Did the crystal bring any issues to the surface for resolution?

....

....

....

....

Did you feel the crystal working in a particular area of your body?

....

Is there any follow-up work needed on any issues brought to light?
What did the crystal teach you about yourself?

....

....

Crystal: ....

Colour, shape, texture and any other notable features:

....

....

....

....

Drawing of your crystal:

Did you programme the crystal or ask it to work in a certain way with you?

....

....

Did you experience any sensations or feelings while working with your crystal?

....

....

....

Did you see any images while using your crystal?

....

....

....

....

....

Did the crystal give you a message?

....

....

....

Did the crystal bring any issues to the surface for resolution?

....

....

....

....

Did you feel the crystal working in a particular area of your body?

....

Is there any follow-up work needed on any issues brought to light?
What did the crystal teach you about yourself?

....

....

FINAL WORD

Congratulations on completing *The Crystal Healing Journal* and for the self-discoveries you've made along the way.

It's beneficial to work with crystals or meditate with them for a few minutes every day, but the pace of modern life can mean this isn't always possible. Rest assured that your crystals will always step up when you need them to, and you can call on them at any time.

You can keep *The Crystal Healing Journal* as a record of your progress, referring back to it whenever necessary to remind yourself of all you've learned so far.

Allow this book to be the springboard for your continued crystal practice and may your healing journey be filled with love and light.

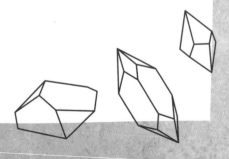

THE LITTLE BOOK OF CRYSTALS

Astrid Carvel

978-1-78685-959-4

Crystals have long been used for holistic healing purposes. Every crystal emits vibrations, which can help to bring balance, calm and positivity into your life. This guide will teach you how to select and maintain your crystals, along with basic techniques for crystal meditation and balancing your chakras, to bring harmony to mind, body and spirit. Discover over 40 crystals, their unique properties and how to make use of their power in everyday life.

THERE IS A CRYSTAL FOR EVERY OCCASION.

Have you enjoyed this book?
If so, find us on Facebook at **Summersdale Publishers**,
on Twitter at **@Summersdale** and on Instagram at
@summersdalebooks and get in touch.
We'd love to hear from you!

www.summersdale.com

IMAGE CREDITS